Drinking
from the River

Other works by Chip Dameron

PROSE

From Ben Bulben to the Rhine

POETRY

In the Magnetic Arena

Night Spiders, Morning Milk, Definition of Hours

Hook & Bloodline

Greatest Hits: 1975 – 2000

Tropical Green

Waiting for an Etcher

Drinking from the River

New & Selected Poems

1975 – 2015

Chip Dameron

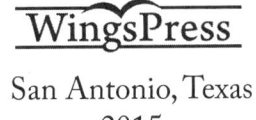

WingsPress

San Antonio, Texas
2015

Drinking from the River: New & Selected Poems, 1975-2015
© 2015 by Chip Dameron

Cover photograph © 2015 by Bruce Jordan. Used by permission.

ISBN: 978-1-60940-473-4 (paperback original)

E-books:

ePub: 978-1-60940-474-1
Mobipocket/Kindle: 978-1-60940-475-8
Library PDF: 978-1-60940-476-5

Wings Press
627 E. Guenther
San Antonio, Texas 78210
Phone/fax: (210) 271-7805
On-line catalogue and ordering:
www.wingspress.com

Wings Press books are distributed to the trade by
Independent Publishers Group
www.ipgbook.com

Library of Congress Cataloging-in-Publication Data

Dameron, Chip, 1947-
  [Poems. Selections]
  Drinking from the river : new & selected poems, 1975-2015 / Chip Dameron.
     pages cm
    ISBN 978-1-60940-473-4 (pbk. : alk. paper) -- ISBN 978-1-60940-474-1
(epub ebook) -- ISBN 978-1-60940-475-8 (kindle/mobipocket ebook) -- ISBN
(invalid) 978-1-60940-476-5 (library pdf)
  I. Title.
  PS3554.A4835A6 2015
  811'.54--dc23
                          2015012601

Again for Joan

Contents

From *Tropical Green*

New Poems

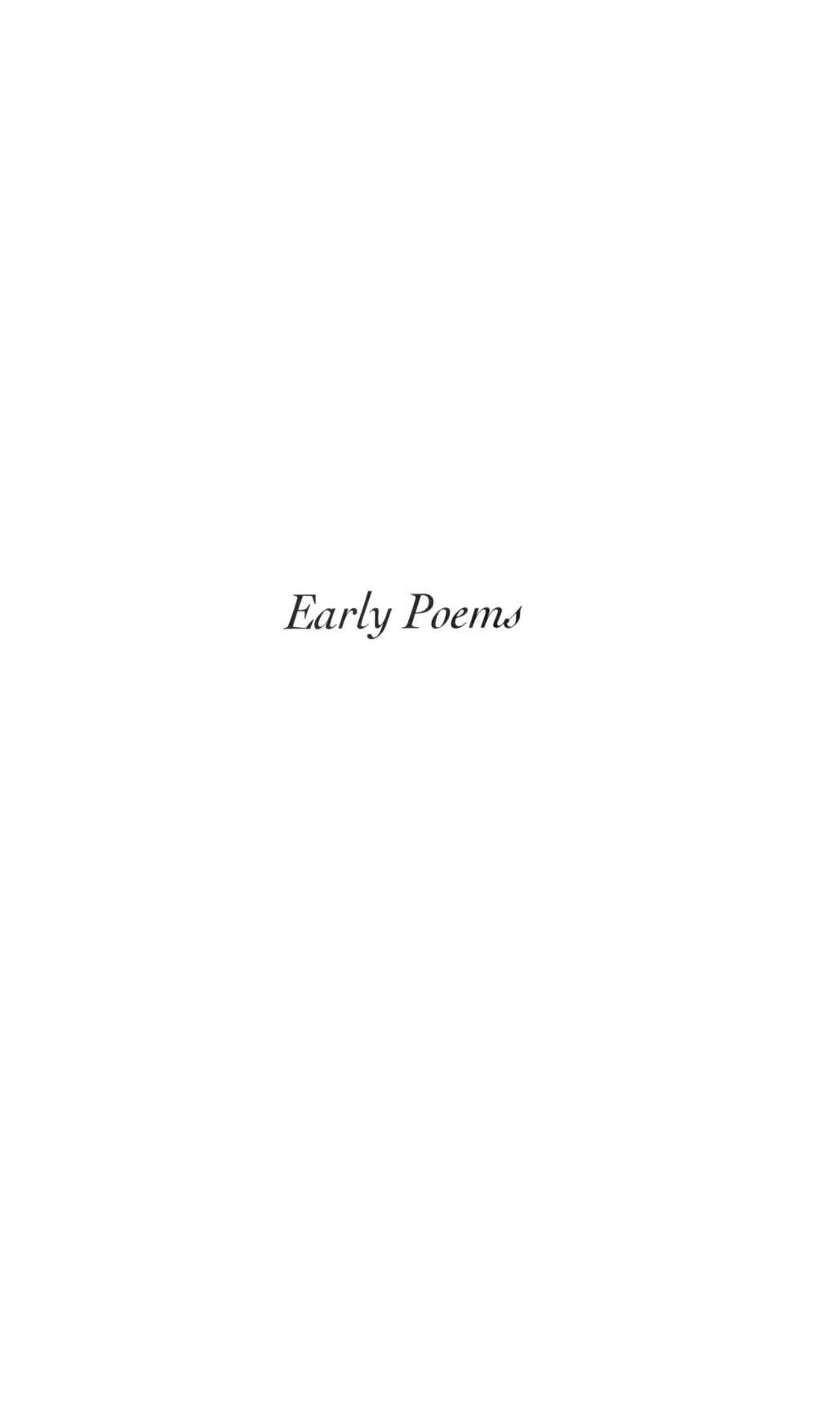

Early Poems

Fiery Beast

Our hefty armor has corroded;
our damsels merely feign distress.
Arthur's noble table was split
for common kindling long ago.
What fiery beast lurks in the foothills
of everyone's fragrant faeryland?

Doppelganger

For years I have balanced
your coffin on my shoulders
and counted on your resurrection
to establish my natural identity.
Tonight I bury you so that
both of us may live, and find ourselves.

The flying dragon in the sky
circles upon itself and turns
on the world's light.
I taste his blood and carry
his fire in my skin as I recast
ordinary shapes and movements.

Shadows in Our Landscape

In the interaction of mind and word
blooms an image, perhaps clear,
perhaps unfleshed and fuzzy,
like sound on a foggy morning
in Georgia or England, or at sea.

Where the image leads is the mind's play,
choosing from a pinwheel of paths.
The choice, though instantaneous,
can be modified and turned, like
a magician's coin, into a fluttering bird.

If the bird is faithful to its flight
we willfully defy our retinal etchings
and watch it hover, hover, then dive,
as if, somewhere in a forgotten dream
or moment from the past, the bird
has been a shadow in our landscape.

Some Balance Is at Stake

Quick nights give way to weeks of sun
in Texas, in August. Things take
their goings slow, or risk the stun

of unpent heat, whose blast can bake
the earth into a shattered pane.
So people turn to beer and lake

for respite; cranky kids complain.
It seems some balance is at stake –
grass yellows, life takes on its stain.

September's no better: days break
out of the dark dry as parched grain.
Then the skyline blackens; winds wake

the dust and drive the drops they've spun;
coolness descends on rock and snake;
dreams lengthen; October's begun.

Between Fouettés

Between the prima ballerina's third
and fourth fouettés: light cracked a silent sheet
of lake into a flood of slivers toward
some town whose wrinkled former mayor, short-
winded lately, just felt a stab of breath
deny his life's inertia; miles away
his plump great-granddaughter began her bath
with one small fisted splash and shrieking *why*;
the audience, transfixed and hushed, all stared
through dazzling solid shafts which seemed to pierce
the tapestry of sound and let the stored
up frozen spinning dancer's art disperse
 – except Suzanne, who sat self-mesmerized,
reshaping touch and smile, slightly aroused.

from **Versepoints to Lawrence Durrell's**
The Alexandria Quartet

   Clea to Darley:

How can men be such pigs? The day
Narouz died – have you heard? – he screamed
my name to hold his death at bay;
and I, hard at my abstract, seemed
on the verge of catching form when
Nessim phoned. "You can hear his groans,"
he said. "Come quick." Disgusted, I then
left. But my flesh quailed on my bones.

   Darley to Clea:

And yet you never saw him. The dike
had broken; water sheered the road
as if it were a ribbon. Like
a stranded sailor, you still owed
an unpaid debt to one who had
departed. How can you deny
that his distorted love, though sad
and spurned, is still a valid cry?

   Clea to Darley:

It was his cry that plagued my thought
in Alexandria; a sound
impalpable but real. I ought
to have sensed something when we found
his island, and his fierce harpoon.
And those foresaken sailors – I
should have guessed they'd bode ill fortune.
Clearly they were his evil spies.

While you were hacking at my wrist
after the accident, his call
caressed my ears; I longed to twist
away, then, and shed for once all
vestiges of self. Not Clea,
but a graceful seabird, at peace,
soaring beyond form and idea.
And you were thwarting that release!

from In the Magnetic Arena

from **A Picasso Montage**

Paints, textiles, inks, metals,
stones, woods, and common objects –
matter enough for the molding,
for the vital transformations
that the keen creator finds
in the corridors of the night.

Self-Portrait (1907)

The eyes – enormous ovals that hold
black pupils locked to the canvas,
that pull us into the angularities
and ovals of an African mask
gone Spanish. They are the eyes
of a magician, of a hunter
who never blinks, of a sailor
on watch in the heart of the night.

Girl before a Mirror (14.3.1932)

The mirrored self,
in its brazen colors
and displaced features,
embodies an imagination.
The silent girl,
whose crossed eyes
dominate a lunar desert,
stands in geometric fullness
against a garish
diamond wallpaper.
The controlled confusion
of color, form, and image
creates her self-satisfaction.

Portrait of a Painter after El Greco **(22.2.1950)**

The original, still hanging
in Franco's Seville, comes to him
through print or photograph.
Sharp, somber, and elusive,
the face becomes a cubist mask
with cat whiskers and firm jaw.
The fingers writhe like silver snakes
and nip at all the brushes.
Poised like a persistent cat
with a lush silver collar,
the painter contemplates his kill.

Villa with Pigeons (**14.9.1952**)

Landscapes sometimes beam
as children do,
full of themselves,
full of a parent's affection.
Coaxed into conception,
this whitewashed villa
links the ice-blue pond
and snowbound back yard
with the summer meadow
of green and gold in front –
alpine and somewhat oriental.
Just outside the canvas
a small boy sits
under laden trees
and watches several pigeons
circle the red roof.
As they flap, he beams.

Self-Portrait (**1901**)

The rim of the night
sparkles with a patina of ice.
At the outset of a long walk,
the painter acknowledges
his stark image in the window
of a dusty, nameless shop.
The body within the dark overcoat
is young and strong,
but the face is pale and cold,
composed and suddenly ageless –
except the eyes, tired
and restless, which turn
image into memory,
memory into vision,
vision into eerie incarnation.

Corrida (7.2.1957)

The impeccable strokes
of a Zen masterpiece. . .
the stark congruity
of a Rorschach blot. . .
bull, horse, and picador,
exploding with energy. . .
the lance, sinking
into the bull's back,
impales the picador;
the rearing horse,
catalyst in this confrontation,
will get its belly slashed.
Nothing remains unbloodied,
nothing remains safe
in the heat of the corrida,
in the terrible black ink
of blood, froth, and sweat
that gives the snow-white page
its frozen beauty.

Jacqueline Roque (**9.10.1954**)

A wicker rocker frames the scarf,
dark and knotted at the throat,
which frames the pale young face.
Her composure transcends time.
She is the mistress, the last great
love, the gentle emissary
of death, who waits outside.
She will become Picasso's
plastic source, and she
will bury him when he dies,
at last, leaving his circus behind.

Picasso's death (8.4.1973)
met me in Mexico City.
His life, long and joyous,
meets me everywhere.

Tones for a Ballet

Red on white on black:
in deep silence
fire and ice
anticipate creation.

Alone, light
makes a magic
circle of itself.

Fire's flicker
grows into glow,
spirals in swirls,
leaps into light,
turning to bright
frozen flame.

Ice stretches,
splits into shards,
explores extremities,
spins into light,
leaps like sea spray,
whirling, whirling
into solid stability.

Fire and ice
fill the magic
circle with consequence.

Motion suggests contact
in the magnetic arena,
in the hurricane's eye.

Tentative interaction
blooms into harmony.
Tension and catharsis
heartbeat the glow
of twining elements.

The circle sings
with subtle virtuosity.

Fire rainbows
the ice pillar's pose,
re-forms into vibration,
spins into sudden
frozen flame.

Fire and ice
melt into deep
silence; light
fills the magic
circle with itself.

This Artifact

This artifact is as hard and distinct
as Yorick's skull. Self-contained and grinning,
it remains after the climactic act –
after the oven, the fistful of pills,
the final bottle, the shotgun's long gaze,
roulette on the freeway, the leap at sea.
It is a tangible account of all
that is mysterious, intangible.
It moves; it doesn't move. This artifact
is an oxygen mask and a tombstone.

A Cannibal, Reading for Orals

The goddamn wind announces this feast
as if it were concerned with either of us.
I have tasted your succulent flesh
and traced its fragile emanations
that cling to stuff like stubborn roots.
I have chewed on the biggest bones
of your body and turned them into weapons.
Your heritage, the common symbol,
surrounds me in its various abstractions.
As I now wiggle at the stake,
your chuckling escalates into frenzy.
Take me in turn with a loving bite
and spit my spirit into the wind.
When the morning comes we can crack
our skulls together and start brush fires
in the dense woods and tinder cities.
When the day is spent we can loaf
in the dark and rekindle our affections.
After our consummation in fire,
we will float, disembodied, into the void.

Pass the Pepper

for Jonah, Ahab, and Pinocchio

Deep in the white whale's belly,
you fritter away your matches
on wet wood, saving the last
for carving on the moving walls.
Now it is dark, and we can
read neither the whale's belly
nor your mind as you sit
in the shallow slosh of juices
and odd objects. Someone
make the whale sneeze. Please!
Someone make the whale sneeze.

Whales on the Wing

At sea the whales hump the waves
and sneer at boats of predators.
The air is thick with alien smells.
To survive they dive deep,
threading the improbable peace
of regions of inexpressible horrors,
ghastly enough in a gob's imagination.
Malevolence bobs on the surface
like a string of persistent buoys.
Suddenly the sea explodes with sound,
and splintered wood slivers the sun
before littering a line toward the horizon.
Picked bones filter to the bottom.
The whales disappear into the sky,
and an early moon tugs at its lover.

On a Still Day

The sky is too blue for miracles.
Framed by it, a sun-kissed limestone
crypt houses vast collections
of manuscripts and memorabilia.
A live oak's green leaves pull sky
and building to the dark earth
where, deep in the hum of silence,
earthworms ferret out the words
that once arched the heavens
and eat them, one by one,
with smacks and farts, for lunch.

When They Keep Coming

Everything she owns
has multiplied.
It might be night
all day, except
that the phone
never stops ringing.
Her stomach twists
into a fist.

The booze she drinks
to soothe herself
is eating its way,
slowly, toward
the open air, where
death is a fact
and life a brief
but curious fiction.

Paranoia

The fleas are only incidental agents
of the grand conspiracy that holds
your house in its invisible grip.
The trees rustle with impatience,
while tentacles of trailing vines
intrude through a bedroom window
and search the air for victims.
Birdie will be the first to go,
poisoned by flies and slowly choked
off its perch by a descending vine.
Some days later the dog will disappear
and her old fleas will grow more vicious,
weaned on the strength of aerosol sprays.
Walter will be next; held down
and splayed across the yard like Gulliver,
he will hear his joints pop apart
and the grass will swallow him whole.
You will be alone in the quiet house,
alone and trembling, awake
from transfusions of coffee and fear,
waiting for the walls to cave in,
waiting for the door to burst open
from the press of grinding insects,
waiting for the furniture to turn
on you and suddenly attack.

Dear Emily

When the moon hid behind a bank
of clouds you stepped right out, calmly,
and streamed into the night, ghost-like.

By living like a cloistered nun
for fifteen years, and wearing white,
as if your lover were coming

any moment for the binding
rights, you'd loosed the town's longest tongues
and given mystery a name.

Then, flaunting that reputation,
you circled the new church's plot
before gliding home, in shadows.

Or so they say, in their musty
correspondence. A local myth
revealed at night in the moonlight.

We find you hiding in poems,
now, and sense, behind you Donnean
conceits, awkwardly correct snips

of diction, and calibrated
focus for ecstasy and pain,
a fierce will for recognition.

Cleat Marks on the Corridor Floor

If you hadn't been a tomboy once
with your hair stuck under
a baseball cap and an even swing
that made the guys down the block
respect you as a ballplayer,
then you'd be just another
disadvantaged woman on the field
now, twenty years later.
Your peppered hits and
tough base-running surprise
your smug, pot-bellied colleagues
who are daily accustomed
to your graceful sweep
through academic halls,
and who may remember that
you spent a dozen years
in a starchy nun's habit
before re-emerging, like
a pale lemon butterfly,
into the slow richness
of the sun's temporality.
It is good that you body
such unexpected complexities
as you move, peripatetically,
toward fullness.

Gift for a Driven Friend

When your pain drives you to plaster
the night with martinis and spook
a crowded room with frozen laughter,
I would give you something elemental:
a chunk of rock, a bowl of water,
a breath of wind that bites with cold.
I would cover you with the day's leaves
and let the sun investigate your secrets.
I would ask the stars to unmask themselves
and reveal their natural energies.
I would present you to the animals.
I would leave you in the wilderness
and let the drumbeats of your wrists
lead you to the cave of your birth.
There you might tend a steady fire
with the sudden cries of the night
and watch for the inevitable forms
that vibrate in the grey dawn –
immobile agents of the sun,
waiting to be named and specified.

To a Blue Horse in South Dakota

There you lean, wading the road
in the blue light of the moon,
far from these green Texas trees.
I smell the fear in the air,
hanging like humidity,
as you breast what the rest
of us would turn from.
Here, closer to the clouds,
I hear of your headway
from the birds that spiral
down to their jeweled nests,
bearing facts in their beaks.
Their lies confuse the leaves.
All I can count on
is your blue coat, steady
between waves, shedding
the blue road and the blue night,
moving still into the blue light
of dawn.

Letters to a Generation of Friends

1

Dear Bill: Suppose the stones
of the cold white buildings
had turned the purple
of the temples at Tenochtitlan,
stinking day and night
of only death. Suppose
our steaks had gone rotten,
the scotch had evaporated,
and rats had eaten the bedding.

That was in another country,
or in Chicago. In Washington
the cops were all too black
to serve as surrogates.
We sat near them at breakfast;
later, their graven features
loomed from plexiglass masks.
The chilled air contained our spirit.

The night was full of food,
of fire, of five or six
Saturday marchers in the nexus
of the telling. As steaks
spit and bled into the grill,
and smoke layered our language,
the war limped back
to its anonymous bodies of water,
to its serpentine illusions.

2

Dear Paul: Tonight I am at home
with silence. The week's work,
a long midwifery in the service
of our groaning tongue, cries everywhere.
All births are laced with blood.
Tonight I will tinker with the space
between syllables, cutting the air
into the shapes of nameless things
that slowly move toward sound.

Alone in your cluttered study,
among the stolid books of law
and dated maps and charts
stained with rain water and whiskey,
you puff on your seasoned calabash
and cloud the windows
with curling Cavendish designs.
And then the room disappears.

The campus never changes.
Everyone is there, waiting for us
to arrive with the worn football.
Grasso at quarterback, Severson
and Banks at ends. The sun
waits above the cold pines.
The faces on the clock tower stop.
Not even the pebbles stir
as we walk the road to the field.

3

Dear Greg: In the photograph
her hands cradle her wan face.
Her arms scar the dozing air,
and photographs on either side
ooze out of all recognition.
Her eyes are the coagulation
of Christ's blood, the strange
and clotted fruit of every cross
that lies across her back.

I can leave this exhibition
and listen to her sing
the slow clarinet of her life,
held surely to the track
by the needle that turns
her closer to the hollow
sound at the center
of her gnawing silence.

In her singing is the pain
and the absence of pain,
the thing that is too much
for body to bear, flesh
stripped of all pretensions,
cells burned away like
dry underbrush. What remains
is the glow of a single tree,
clear and violent, at night.

4

Dear Robert: On those long trips
that seamed the girth of the South,
when food would turn tasteless
and churn in our stomachs,
talk held us to the road, shaped
the rolling landscape, tuned
our loyalties. There are trips
we should still take, naming
the towns as we find them.

I could delineate the places
around Durham that we filled
with conversations – the Donut Dinette,
the Ivy Room, Mayola's, the Rat,
Annamaria's, the Blue Light, Bullock's,
the Zoom-Zoom Room, the Palms.
We measured our lives with beer,
plate lunches, cigarettes, coffee.

On weekends I waited for women
to dive into my bobbing heart
and satisfy its roiling verberations.
You cast a treble tongue
that pulled them, one by one,
into the dizzy smell of flesh.
Afterwards, a wading in bloody waters.
The signatures of their toes
were stricken by the first hard storm.

5

Dear Steve: Are you writing tonight,
with wife tucked under a grandmother's
quilt? So I hear, so I can imagine.
The night air, raw and purpled,
sings bitterly into the chimney.
The gas stove conjures everything:
ship, wardroom, tense watches
on the bridge, attack planes
slung wearily into the endless fog.

I remember less. Technical terms
stuck to my transient LPD like
barnacles – I came ashore
stripped of my obligations.
But not the salt film
on the signal bridge, the sound
of the cloven sea, the rolling
basketball games in the hold.

Now, as Supervisor of Diction,
I plead for particularities.
In these cold rooms,
where silence hangs like meat
in a cut-rate butchery,
words are blades of ice
that stick to the tongues
of stone animals or fall
to the floor like feathers.

6

Dear Hargraves: We wonder
where you've been. I concentrate
on the shape of your teeth,
the shape of your wide smile,
Long Island in your diction.
You walked out of my live
wearing sneakers. I find
old cigarette butts, old records,
old books about the Beats.

I stand in a cold room
in Durham and wait for you
to arrive. The radiator
organizes the loose silence.
Someone above begins dribbling
a basketball. I watch
a candle absorb the room,
then gutter across the linoleum.

The night bends behind the trees.
Is it getting late?
I am rebuilding this room
out of everything I have saved.
The walls are taped together.
Music curves from one corner.
The pipe goes back and forth,
slower and slower, and the only
thing above us is the sky.

7

Dear Vick: Who is off the line
and in motion, somewhere
between the long yardlines,
digging through the grass,
straining for the hard-edged ball.
Now Who leaps into the sky,
slicing it with a scimitar's
quick and able cleaving,
and hangs in the cool air.

Who watches it gather mass
as if to stun the earth.
Who waits for the explosion,
arms open, eyes locked
to the spot on the sun
that is as big as the world.
Who remains in mid-air,
in motion; moments pass.

Who is in motion and is not
in motion, the ball curving
out of its awesome arc
and the sky falling away.
Sound comes to a standstill.
Who waits and is waiting
in the crisp air, alone,
as the ball comes, is coming,
true to its turning skin.

8

Dear Betty B: The first was such
a different campus – more formal,
coolly monasterial, its flying
spires sending education heavenward.
Everything glowed with passions
held in check, like bold horses
bolting from their stables,
bit-bloodied but partially free,
cuffing the sweet grass into clumps.

The other, its spatter of buildings
the sun-baked teeth of its smile,
humored our serious inclinations.
All summer, academia cooled
its nouns in Lake Travis
and pared adjectives to the bone.
During the other nine months
everything verbed energetically.

Our friends are having children.
I imagine that you must
at least be pregnant, worrying
a bit about weight, counting
your days carefully. Those years
we spent in hot house purgatories
line our veins and, one hopes,
prepare our bloods for the partings
that will, like falling angels, come soon enough.

9

Dear Frank: Perhaps there's time
for a portrait. The artist
sits at the easel's pleasure.
The paints make their marks,
one by one; the neck extends,
the eyes come clear, the nostrils
twitch. The thin hands,
cupped loosely at the crotch,
do not need to move.

The canvas is a canvas
and a slender man.
The artist will remain
inside the canvas, waiting
to become its texture,
while the paints conspire
with quick fibs
and lurid fabulations.

Either the background seethes
with obscene implications
as the artist meditates;
or the luminous figure,
wet and phallic,
consecrates an evening sea;
or all divisions evaporate
and the world turns white.
The canvas is complete.

10

Dear Prissy: Imagine a painting
full of movement at its dark center,
the edges freezing into a lemon
halo that suggests beatification.
A face stretches across a canvas,
its features twisted into a frenzy
of calcined umber ropes.
It spits soundlessly at grace,
at whatever gleams into the night.

The painting has been harboring
someone's vision. It watches us
prowl about and fix our sights
on its intricate persuasions.
Its veins rush like bulging rivers.
It leads to the sea, to the rocks
beside the sea, their chins
jarring the waves that pound in.

Something swims beyond the surf
and knifes into the thick blueness.
Our teeth begin to ache from all
the tuna that we have eaten
in our dreams. Late at night,
we count the fish in the sky.
At dawn, like a steady sun,
the painting rises from the sea,
slowly, its colors foaming.

11

Dear John: In a small town
in Mexico a guitar calls out
to the moon. The song
might be the same from night
to night, a dog's howl
across the cactus plain, the same
intonation as tomorrow's, when
the guitar, tuned or untuned,
will turn away from its woodenness.

The men sweat out their beer
and idle talk. It is enough,
now, to hear the thin guitar
as it warps the spattered walls
and leaves the room behind,
its notes articulating a landscape,
while the men sleep alone
or alongside their dreaming women.

In the morning the men hear
the rooster's rasp, the cart's creak,
the *sssst* of a young dog
pissing against a stucco wall.
The guitar, propped against a chair,
plays on. Throughout the town
the staggering day wakes
to resume its domination,
its noises flexing with sunlight.

12

Dear Francie: In my Chinese room
I enter the forest like a deer.
Everything is moving. The sounds
of leaf and bird and stream
begin to slow my striding
toward a twin across the clearing.
I close my eyes and am on
a mountain, at daybreak, on skis.
The sky sits down with me for tea.

If you had seawater in your veins
and a mountain in your heart,
when would you sail and when would you climb?
Under this white sun, talk withers.
Are vegetables more real than words?
Your garden is a long organic novel
in the timeless comic tradition –
Tom Jones told by a ripe tomato.

I have forgotten which movie I am in –
is this a scene with the Whole Sick Crew?
Why is Anais Nin reading from her diary?
Who are the women with Henry Miller?
Someone gave me a script with photographs
instead of words, and each was a study
of your face. When I asked for you
they said you were directing Dylan
in a movie on the curse of fame and fortune.

Hard Labor

　　　　　　　Above all,
there must be movement in the play
of pale symbols torn from the air
and wrestled into some temporal
sequence.
　　　　　　　Everything must almost
leave the page, and then, when
the various sounds are straining
against the edge, something
off the page might move as well,
and the brave, ungainly dancer
at center stage becomes invisible
as Nijinsky's ghost redeems the scene
before disappearing with the final note
into the eaves of the wing, carrying
the audience's cheers into the open corners
of the night.

Shepherd in the Moon

                  At night,
deep in our pillows, we see
him circling the perimeter
of our lives.
                  Great white beast,
searching for something that
creases the air with its scent,
he snuffles through the vines,
muscles primed for movement.
Bounding then across the lawn,
he leaps toward the moon
and disappears, suddenly,
without a splash.
                  The sun
covers his trails with green days
and scrubs his haunts
with odorless light.
                  Yet
we see him, white against white,
when the moon rises.

In the Forests, on the Waves

                          Something
moves in the blood, like knowledge,
deeper than self-awareness. It stalks
the heart and makes its inevitable claim,
accurately.
                    What happens in the mind
is something else, the tougher of the two.
It comes and doesn't come, slowly,
a shy doe at the edge of the stream,
anxious and cautious, filtering the sounds
that cleave the air.
                          When hunter
and doe converge, the seams of the sky
split and tons of blue confetti stars
obscure the sun and ride the sea's waves
toward their roiling crests, triumphantly
perilous.

Elephants and Mariachi Music

        Listen to the night
cry out for something it is seeking.
The road through those hills
is dense with movement, and whatever
goes there is lost in the trumpeting
of elephantine ghosts.
                Now
the air freezes into a sheet
of unwritten music. The moon's
envoys interrupt the night's
preoccupations, and everything
deepens into pinlight – the trees
wear black haloes, the birds rustle
like fat undertakers.
                  But crickets
intrude, abruptly, like an unexpected
mariachi band, and as the garish group
ripples through a standard number,
strummed and hi-hied, the night retreats
to our corner table and settles down
to drink.

A Cat's Lunar Discovery

                    Come.
It is as a cat that you hold
to the edge of my territory,
hackle-hardened, stark and still.
Your dilated eyes expand
the room's dimensions, and the walls
change from white to blue.
                              I wish
I had such long and accurate whiskers
when night sets in and the eyes strain
for shapes and movements.
                              The slow
swish of your tail is more ambiguous
and precise than language.
                              Draw your claws
and bathe in the telescopic light
of the moon, alone and buried
in dreams that lead, finally,
back to daylight, back to the moon's
hidden surface.

From

Night Spiders, Morning Milk,
Definition of Hours

Place of Alphabets

       Who knows
how we came to be
awake in this place
of alphabets, where
the Ts provide a bit
of shade and the Rs
all rush downhill,
searching for an S
and the promise
of plurality.
          Close
your eyes and listen
to the clock deep
in your vowels, where
tick and tock tell
it all.
      The air
is for stringing
a song, the wind
is for twisting it
around the contours
of our lives, where
we sort through
the endless cackle
of consonants.

Home Cooking

                    Ah,
to make a poem as red
and as spicy as a plate
of *asado de puerco* –
to grind out the verbs
for body, to trim
each noun of its fat,
to spoon the sounds
onto a fresh tortilla:
the most ravenous mind
would burp with pleasure.

Man Who Lives among Birds

for José Marcelo Garza

                    Friend,
when great-tailed grackles
float down and strut
around my yard, eyes
imperious, aflicker, I think
of you at your house,
still by window or porch,
the wet birds preening
among the sprinkler heads,
their glint of midnight blue
sparking your day.
                         In class,
after you've read a poem
by Frost or Dickinson,
a bird stands fixed against
the page, and no one knows
what sound it makes or
where it would be going
could it go at all.
Then someone sees a word
begin to flutter, a line
begin to rise, a black
shape in search of itself,
its eye on fire, its beak
searing all sense as it
shatters a window and speeds
into the dark that waits
outside.

Boston Blueblood, Southern Drawl

      All the skunks
are out tonight, Cal –
they cross the highways
of their dreams, dodging
the white glare of careening
eyes, loosing their stink
against this arrogant metallic
invasion.
                Yes, perhaps
more salt would have kept
you mellow. You paid for
that involuntary euphoria,
a horse beyond the bit,
beyond the road, caught up
in the lonely clatter of
falling hooves.
                  Somewhere
in this part of the woods
are the terms of correspondence,
waiting to spring into
a clearing and turn kinetic,
their muscled excellence
as true as the fittest violin,
tuned to your unexpected drawl,
where words trail on and off,
as strange and as ordinary
as *coffee*.

Dry Season

                    Standing
in the thicket of her heart:
light licking up the leaves,
sky like water, wind absorbing
sound. The smell of dusk
on her branches could buckle
your breath. On the day
the animals spooked their shadows
and evaporated, trees twisted
from the truth, their roots
aquiver.
                    When words
in the air lost all moisture,
no one was there to give
them their heft, their swell,
their labial bops and mambos.
No one else heard the fizzle
of the fricatives as they slid
through the brush, sparking
the twigs for tinder, crackle
and smoke and heat taking
the sear to its limits,
scorching life back to the bone,
back to its driest whiteness,
back to its most selfish self.

Toward Home

            The day
still dark, the rustling wind
and a lone dog's bark
so clear I can see them,
nearly, sounds I'd like
to scrape from the trunk
of a tree and stuff into
my pocket, sure to want
them should the buzzing get
unbearable.
                The dashboard
glows like a clouded moon.
Beyond the wheel, everything
out there takes its broken
bearing, fixed in this web
of correspondence.
                    Like boys
going home from night fishing,
flashlights bobbing, my car
takes the park road over
to the highway. I look
both ways and just go,
no matter left or right,
up a hill and straight
toward the bluing day,
ready to come round
a bend and be there,
light in the window, food
and coffee going, taking
hold of flesh that burns

and heals, both, like tar
on an old patched road,
bubbling in the sun.

From

Hook & Bloodline

Hook and Bloodline

            Knee deep
in South Bay, spinning out
an artificial shrimp
to hook a speckled trout
or drum, you watch the terns,
fixed on fish, dive
like newsreel Zeros at dusk,
smacking the air with their
wallops, each white bird
rising from the froth
of an airplane's fatal
plunge, another sea
and forty years away,
still potent.
                All night long
the ships rolled to port
and starboard, the men
banked into bunks, dreaming
of women and death,
no convoy safe in the zone
of paranoia, the deep
as cunning as the sky.
On watch, the loudspeaker's
squawk as close as humid air,
the men calmed their coffee
with whispers and waited out
the worst.
            Elsewhere
a city bloomed and withered
in a moment, the sky as bold
as love, the wind more violent
than any lust. Flesh fell off.

Things writhed in their wombs.
Days later, another dose
of the same.
      When the sailors
came back, fit and unfearful,
their salty tongues as quick
to snatch at sweetness
as a snake's, the cries
in the darkness were most
of what mattered, some nights
never long enough. By day,
life became suburban,
televised, circumnavigated
by kids.
      Now, far from home
and childhood, flounder gig
at ready in the hissing
lantern light, you slog
along the shallows, looking
for the dark shapes that hover
by the bottom, stunning them
by spear, taking the firm
white flesh for yourself,
the heat of the fire
searing in a truth
that you taste each time
you chew with the teeth
of your faceless godparents,
whose vapors still hang
in the air.

Grandad's Campfire

                    Is it down
this way, down beyond
those scrub mesquites,
down where the road curves
out of sight, taking
its barbed argument along
for company?
                    Somewhere
out here, long before
blindness and age rode
him into a rocker, Grandad
slept in the open, sheep
nearby, and daydreamed
of Annie, his spunky wife
back home.
                    No one
can tell me much more,
more than the claim
that he damn near died
once, some malady or other
pressing him to the cot
in an isolated lineman's
shack, sweated out at last
alone.
                    Some of it's
in books, but they don't
smell like horse sweat
and cornbread. Maybe
at the bottom of the hill
I'll see a camp, a fire,
some dogs, and listen
as the bleats define the dark.

Maybe when I'm close enough
to speak, he will nod toward
the three-legged stool
and fill another tin cup
with coffee.

Grandma's Anecdote

           Tough
as country gossip, she lived
off oil-field gases and stumped
around her house,
                but here,
under a tent and speechless,
she'd gulp down oxygen
and finally go,
                no match
for the rumor that bored
into her story and sucked
the verbs dry,
                leaving the rest
to blow like tumbleweeds
across West Texas.

Fat Love

Ten years ago
our love was fat against
the bone, sweet and all
aquiver, quick to burn
but quicker still to stretch
against the skin's lean
life.
      These days, mostly
muscle holds us where we've
come to, flexed, firm,
efficient in its twitching,
taking us together to the
open doorway and the road
beyond.
          In moments when
we let this living go,
I can still find the fat,
smell its oily incense,
watch it swell and engulf
us, turning outside inside
inside out.

Tree House Song

        Mornings,
floating in bed among
the branches of these
ebonies, you become
the song of a bird
that has reached what
it's been looking for,
here in this leafless
room, and I hold
each note in my heart
until it dies, taking
a piece of the dark
along with it.
        Later,
when light has come on
to delineate limb from
limb, house sparrows
pulse back and forth
from tree to bougainvillea,
and we climb down
to move among the sounds
of this city, the bird's
song still an echo
in my veins.

The Song That Ends the Night

        Here inside
this midnight house of heartbeats
comes a sudden ping of sound,
one note at a time,
             accelerating
slowly into a tumbling wave
of foaming rhythms, thrashing
contrapuntally against the reefs
of the mind, overwhelming until
the first pulse of light thins
the air, spreading like a desert,
cold and particulate,
            molding
sound against each waking shape,
the twang absorbed, palm tree
and car and coffee pot astir,
voices making this the choir
that brings to life the searing,
fateful song that each of us has
just been waiting for.

Toward the Crux of an Illusion

             I lie in bed
during those moments before
the day begins in earnest,
hearing the surf at the reef,
hearing some mosquito circle
with a vengeance, the green coil
gone ashen cold. Downstairs,
floorboards creak, toilets flush,
water boils, kerosene lamps
illuminate the conversation
that flickers lightly across
the ceiling.
             At night, in bed
again, with some French movie
pulsing from the television's
only channel in the darkened room
below, I enter a printed world
of islands just verging toward
mystification, the people
pausing at the shoreline to watch
the great ships fill the harbor,
the unspoken prospects of commerce
and salvation pounding arrhythmically
against the cool skin of descending
dusk.
             Later, the night begins
to uncoil its variegated dream –
green islands turn yellow and blue,
lagoons are a maze of weed
and coral huts, men knife into
the air and fill their lungs
with the sounds that women

have hung there. Boot marks
on the beach just deepen each time
the tide comes in.
                        As dawn
blinks this all into some astral
oblivion, I return to the angles
of my room, mute and uncharted.

Perilous Epiphany

What can old men do?
Bewhiskered, befuddled, awash
in the stinking wake, watching
that fat ship wallow dockward;
then those dapper gents,
whiter than sin, geysering
champagne, luring our maids
up the gangway, the hollow
thwocks of their shimmering tails
no music to take the measure
of our mermanhood, surely.
                              Aye,
let them loll about all afternoon
and lust for the evening's
final crescendo – let them stew
in their oaths as they yearn
for pliant thighs, rubbing
themselves bloody against
those unforgiving scales, while
we slit the lines, fin quick,
tow the ship seaward, and set
it spinning, our maids beginning
their immemorial crooning
as they arc overboard, teasing
those dandies into following,
the swirling sea sucking
those lubbers down its throat
like so many cheap oysters
at happy hour. Let the lessons
of this watery world adhere
like barnacles to their bones.

Gauguin in Eden: Koke at Mataiea

Easel by palm,
beach by tide, blue by mountain:
the light leans unblinking
as the breeze brings the place
to life, the sound of clattering leaves
almost lost in the surf forever,
the men swinging their silver fish,
strung on vines, over the rim
of their beached pirogue.
Teha'amana
stands in the doorway, green pareu
knotted loosely at the neck, a smile
as shy as childhood coming and going
like a bird's trill, tongue licking
one corner of her mouth.
He thinks
it's fine to be thirteen, or forty-four,
no matter, as long as he can smell
the dark lushness of the jungles
that are rooted in the humus
of his mind, finding those totems
that bring back a red and orange world
that has no factual existence, but comes
as quickly as shadows do, as shadows
turn the night into the thing
the day yearns for, intensely without form,
without color, humid with emotion.

The Promise of Paradise

                    Lost
and now found, that taste
of perpetual summer sticks
to our lips like the sea
itself, its sirens bronze
with innocence, the stonefish
on the floor of the lagoon
too clearly visible to be
dangerous.
                    The thing to fear
lurks at the inner edge
of our retinas, where life
has been refracted, upended,
reconstituted, and we zoom in
on fictions of frozen heat.
So as the dance begins, none
notice that, above the flickering
hips, about the generous breasts,
a moonlit skull sucks us into
its blackened holes.

Sense of Place

It tightens more
and more as the months pass.
The road does.
            Its undulating
curves bespeak the slow circumference
of island time: a heft of sameness
in the thickening air, the waves
malevolently tame, the bright spunk
leaching out of the crotons' leaves,
the day overlong.
            Some French ones
feel it worst, those colonial
compatriots in leisure, quick to bare
their features along the lagoon,
irradiating themselves in the sunlight.
When the moon's noose becomes a taste
on the roof of the mouth, though,
they book their flights and go,
those teachers and bureaucrats
and entrepreneurs, they fill their lungs
from the boundless cities of France,
smelling their aboriginal haunts,
relishing the idiomatic flavors
of every overheard conversation,
wondering why the rain sounds the same
on the roofs of the buildings but tastes
different.
            Only when they return
to their homes do they become
entirely themselves, these people
who stand beside their mailboxes

late in the afternoon and drink in
the oily fragrance of the slickened
roadway.

Fishing in Moorea

In the lengthening
afternoon, after the clouds
have massed above the emerald peaks,
peppered everything wet, and moved on,
there is time to enter the lagoon
and motor slowly past the darkened
clots of coral in the shallows.
Ahead, the waves bash the reef;
behind, roofs are disappearing
into the slope's omnivorous
volcanic vegetation.
                        Anchoring
at the reef's inner edge, we cross
its pocked plateau, brace against
the wash from those detonations
just ahead, and cast crosswise
into the swells at the head
of the pass, where jackfish
congregate. We sling our lures
parabolically into the wallowing
troughs between waves, then
jerk and crank, jerk and crank,
dragging our hooks through
an undulating mystery.
                            Arm-wearied,
many casts later, I feel the hook
harden and watch the rod quiver,
then steepen toward this sudden prize.
The fish roils the surface, once, twice,
as I reel in, staggered briefly

by a boiling surge. When the jack
is nearby, and nearly beaten,
my friend lifts the line expertly,
grips the fish in his calloused hand,
and broadly smiles. "C'est bon –
a beeg feesh," he pronounces.
The jack lashes its tail, vainly,
its pastel scales ashimmer in
the declining light.
                              When
we return to the waiting boat,
my two-foot jack, stringered,
flaps in the air. As dusk
comes on, we angle back toward
the shore, motor humming,
happy, a fine fish for tomorrow's
table, taken from the sea
through much exertion, luck,
and surprise. As we glide
through the shallows, I wonder
what hook I am on, what strike
will leave me gulping hard
for air.

Tahitian Cockfighter

                Early yet,
the phantom cocks are floating
like a fragrance in the dark,
all raspy strutting. If Jean-Pierre
weren't a local gendarme, surely
some neighbor would have spurred
the station by now. Cocka-roo!
Cocka-rurra-rurra-roo!
                            Later,
in full sunlight, Jean-Pierre
stands before his caged cocks,
round belly bare and streaked
with sweat, hair slicked back,
big smile shy of several teeth,
hooting and haggling in French
with some Chinese fancier
of blooded spurs.
                        Inside, someone
retells his nightmare: one night,
driving outside of Papeete,
Jean-Pierre struck a stumbling man
on the road but, less drunk than
his luckless victim, sideswiped
blame.
            It is hard to measure
the heart of man or cock,
and his, thumping erratically
through middle age, threatens
to betray him, threatens to deny
his mind and body the simplest
satisfactions that time dispenses,

as if some errant spur will catch
him off guard, its point striking
to the root of his bloodedness,
sticky and salty, turning
his whole world as red as
undiluted pain, quicker than one
can caw.

Herenui

   Every house
or bamboo hut is open
to whatever air brings,
day and night, eves
and doorways screenless,
the girl on the couch
just as splendidly green
and indefinable as leaves
are, waxing in sheens
of light.
     Whenever
she swims, white panties
sheer and crotchwise,
something floats below,
keen and becoraled,
waiting for the sun
to blink, waiting for
her breasts to swell
against the limits
of the skin, waiting
for her kick to send
her skyward, the air
bound to lick her dry,
the day bound to take
the measure of her secret
wounds.

Uncle Ralph

    Cobbled to his house
are the memories of skins
that are no longer near,
smells that are no longer
potent, times that are
no longer told.
               He's come back
to these islands of his birth
to decode his wife's abrupt
divorce. His other island life,
vending tourist stuff in St. Thomas,
spins in dizzied disarray.
Mornings, garbed in his old
boss's silk pyjamas, he munches
toast, swallows coffee, and drifts
among his deficits.
               Last night,
though, at the feast, his thinning
dyed curls bound by a homemade
crown of gorgeous gaudy flowers,
he led a lanky childhood friend
onto the floor, and to the band's
acceleration he waggled his hips,
one arm akimbo, and grinned
effortlessly, in love with every
woman in the group, carefree
and contagious.

Elegy for Billie

      Persisting in her bony
logic, she ordered her world
as if it were free to stop
its busyness, climb onto her back,
and glide with her across
the lagoon's transparent tensions,
her soft brown arms providing
all the power and balance
and grace that such a world
might require.
                Beyond this veranda,
beyond the gray veil of rain
that masks the reef, beyond
the sibling islands, a woman
stands in the surf on a beach
in southern France, ankle deep
in memory, her children nearby,
wet and oblivious: another beach,
another language, another man,
when winter was a metaphor
and youthfulness as much a fact
as the sound of waves against the
guardian reef.
              In the small room
where she used to sew, most afternoons,
the mosquitoes that never bothered
her still float like oversized motes
of dust in the slanting light,
waiting patiently for new blood.
An absence moves around all day,

all night, filling the humid air
with words that are no longer spoken.
Far away, my toddling son, indifferent
to her death, hitches up the skimpy
briefs she stitched for him, rolls
his black Polynesian pupils, and
propels his sturdy golden limbs
toward the plastic wading pool
that fills him with spontaneous,
unlimited delight.

Star Bright

      One year later,
you still seem to remember
those balmy nights when,
after the evening meal
on the wide veranda, flush
with wine and idle talk,
I carried you down the lawn
to the beach and sang you
to sleep, rocking sideways,
stunned by the Milky Way's
splatter against the black sky,
letting the sound of the sea
scrub my thoughts of their
stock preoccupations, drawing
you deep into my lightening
bones.
      Now, half a world
away, you stand on our drive
and say, "Look, Daddy – the moon!
Hold me and sing the song."
As we sway on the pavement,
your arms squeezing my neck,
I close my eyes and sing
softly, off key, an improvisation
on the things that hold us
close, that stretch beyond
this moment, binding sky
and sea and earth, stars
and blooded beings, pulling
us toward some dying flicker
of light.

Game Catch

    The closest thing
to a lie is a moment's
deepest yes: the perfect
dive for a ball off a bat,
the gloved and echoed sting
verifying every hidden wish,
the shift and fling as true
as summer.
            The hum we hear
is just the buzzing of the day's
doings, wind across an infield,
electric lights that click on
and carve out a lifetime,
where line drives up the alleys
can tear holes in the air
that can't be fixed.

Night Ball

      Men in their thirties
take the field, stake out
their positions, spit into gloves,
and lean against the tension
of each pitch, waiting for whatever
will come. As the ball falls
parabolically and the bat
accelerates toward contact, nothing
else is worth a damn.
                  Before
the crisp metallic thwock dies out,
ball looping toward shallow left,
the shortstop turns and sprints
for the spot where the ball
must come down, his radar
as canny as a bat's, glove
outstretched and head rising
at the last moment, star
spinning down through the night's
curving arc of silence, broken
at last by the luminous plunk
in the pocket.
            Tomorrow
these men will be bound
by their offices and shops
and classrooms. Tonight
they prowl across the clay
and grass arena. At bat,
the shortstop licks his chops
and lines the ball deep into
left, fair by no more than a
whisker.

Relay Man

       Somebody drives
the ball through the gap in left
center, and the shortstop drifts
beyond the infield's arc, waiting
for the left or center fielder
to run the ball down and fling it
toward him.
         On the fly or off
a hop, no matter, the thing's
to time the swing back home,
turning and whipping a hard
overhand to the plate, where
the runner from first cannot slide
out of his pending doom, ball
buried in a leather web, ending
the inning.
        At short you live
to make the pivot, you trust
your arm to get it right, this
humming toward home, and lordy
do you let it fly.

The Horse Beside the Road

           Big
as a sideshow fat man,
legs stiff as pickets,
somebody's horse hogged
the shoulder of our suburban
country road and put
its final claim on air
it couldn't breathe.
           So
traffic slowed, this hulk
no dog or cat or luckless
armadillo, crunched or
abruptly kissed goodbye –
the absent car left
everything open as night
came on.
           Pinned against
a crazed concavity, ears
ringing from the dark thump
and a groan that tore
the nerves as it slid across
the sky, these drivers
lost their bearings as
they passed, the road
taking them on and on
and on.

Rendezvous

            Here are Picasso
and Hemingway, sitting in a café,
drinking red wine from musty bottles,
talking about women.
                    When live
bullets nip at their exaggerations,
Hemingway, puffed with grenades
and pistols, nods goodbye and strides
into action.
              Picasso turns the sounds
into the thin lines of a drawing
of a dream. He broods and drinks
from a bottle.
                Hemingway, feeling
his way among the frayed abstractions,
rips his ribs on the bamboo spikes
at the edge of enmity.
                Picasso rises,
crosses the room, opens the door,
and asks the fleeing women to come
inside and pose.
              As the noise subsides,
Hemingway binds his wounds with words
and reinvents his shadow.
                  Late at night,
Picasso attunes his canvas to a scene
in a café: two men, drinking red wine
from musty bottles, talk about women.

The Night's Incision

                  The voices
that you hear are just your own,
my dear, telling you the things
you have been fighting
all along, twisting time
into a pretzeled simulacrum
of the past, where you
have always been your daddy's
Barbie doll, frozen on film,
thin red nightie no correlative
for innocence.
                  Now you turn
against the moment's involutions,
anticipating the first gestures
of dawn, perhaps, wondering
how best to measure the night's
incision, or love's, and by
the twitching of your skin
I gauge the jolts that you
are bound, still bound, to bear.

What Happened to a Man
on His Patio

        As the man
sat in his shorts and sandals
on the patio and waited for
his coffee to cool, he watched
his wife water the overgrown
beds and lifeless hanging baskets
with a pitcher of sunlight, but
when she turned she cooed as
a mourning dove, a choir of doves,
and when she crouched to pull
a weed she flicked her tail
like a slow whip at the other
cats who'd scaled the brick wall
to investigate.
        When the man's
toes turned into eggs and cracked
open, the cats came and lapped up
their breakfast, and the doves
dropped down and snatched at
the seeds that kept bursting
from his fingers, one by one,
as they fell toward the flagstones,
and later, as the cats bathed
themselves in the shade of a tree
and the fat doves nodded along
an overhanging power line, an ant
battalion hustled in and carried off
the crumbs.

Surface Tension

                No one
speaks English here. Men
stalk the forest, take in
dying with each measured breath.
Women pound roots by day,
then open in the deepest dark
like plyers.
                The ground holds
the smell of a thousand animals.
Waiting at the edge of it all,
you wonder if this world
is a thing of sun and earth
and most essential violence.
The trees shiver in the breeze
and click and click.
                        Beyond
the looping vines and tangled
undergrowth, you spot the car
and house and livelihood
that float on the surface
of your dream's undulating
membrane. Thinner than a drum
beat, that dream still vibrates
with two versions of a vain
and immemorial song, the one
you suppose you have always
been singing.

Mountain Song: Rancho del Cielo, Mexico

We've been walking
at angles all morning, here
where the sky hovers above
the tips of towering trees,
far from the linear truths
of the windswept flats of deep
South Texas.
                    Rains come daily,
but fissured limestone leaches
out what isn't snared at once
and saved. Life surges through
the canopy, where bromeliads
festooning trees are the tanks
where salamanders take their
water.
            After lunch, and talk,
clouds roll down the trees like
some god's own urgent breath,
taking each of us into its cool
oblivion, and then an Irish tune
dances down the mist, hummed by
harmonica, and we might be on
the Irish coast, with Yeats,
meditating on old times, old
ways, but as the clouds thin
the tropics come back as
butterflies, and one lights on
the hand of the musician, each
white underwing tattooed with
a perfect 88, and then it's off,

floating toward death like a song
that moves from sunlight into
sorrow.
        We leave early, by
headlight, the air full of wet
earth and the calls of mysterious
birds, and when we reach the road
to the village at the bottom,
we are among young children
and mango orchards and limes
the size of a fist. Soon we
will find our other skins and
put them on again.

Banding near the South
Texas Coast, Late April

                Beak
by wing and weight
by band, oven bird
by chestnut-sided
warbler, forty birds
were netted, numbered,
noted if by chance
someday they're found
in Maine or Manitoba
or Manhattan.
                Better
than small science
was the vireo's white-
eyed stare, the female
cerulean's sea-green
skullcap.
                Best was
Mandy, age thirteen,
letting loose a bunting,
blue flash of life
gone so soon into thick
brush just across the
road.

During Spring Migration

                        We found
a good place to find birds.
On this side of the road,
an oxbow pond harbors heron,
osprey, grebe. On that side,
invisible calls pop out from
a meadow of reeds. Around
the bend, among the scrub
and native trees, we count
warblers, kingbirds, buntings,
orioles. A cuckoo. New life
birds for some. Not quite like
a fallout on the island, trees
full of birds worn down from
crossing the Gulf, but keen
and companionable.
                        As we bird
back toward our cars, we spot
a border patrol van parked
athwart the road, a couple
of agents at work among three
Mexicans sitting in the dirt
who crossed the river again
this morning.

Dipper on the Cuchara River

              Suddenly,
out of the craw of a drainage
pipe that pulls a mountain
stream from under a nearby
road, it rockets forth a foot
above the flow, rapid flap
ablur, then veers downstream
around a bend.
                    I watch it
now, its coal-black shape
half hidden in the fractured,
shadowy light, pulsing to its
own aerobics beat, wings elbowing
up and down, legs pumping at
the knee.
             Then from its wet
rock perch it plunges down into
the icy swirl, walking the bottom
for whatever it can find. All
I see, though, is its absence
from our world, the one we breathe
and breed in, and when I think
it can't come up it does, over
there, bursting into air, skimming
to another rock, apulse again,
tuning into these two worlds
as easily as light flickers in
and out and off a feast of
surfaces.

Kingdom on Earth

            The ducks
are lined up along the resaca,
their quacks as crisp as
the light that lures them
into motion, their waddle
in cahoots with the colors
and sounds that surround
us, awash in the slow flood
of living.
            What can we
say about what it means
to stretch our skin around
the day, when each pore
holds all the water?
                        Walt,
you were windy but you knew,
harbored by the streets
that scuffed the leather
of your heart, how light
against a window could give
a room its sanctity, there
in the noises of the men
who were testifying.

The Reading Room

                    Far bigger
than we need: desks for
forty or fifty. We take
a dozen and circle in
on ourselves.
                    Day by day
we listen to the voices
that break out from the page,
each shard of sound part
of the mystery of why
we gather at all.
                    Maybe
we are sitting by a stream,
hearing as one the rippled
rush of water, again and
again.
          Let us now bless
the ventriloquists who fill
out the room, who give
us the ripened bounty of
their verbing—may we
turn our own tongues into
trumpets and piccolos, may
we tell of what we see
and do not see as we feel
our way along the banks
of our living in the dark.

From

Tropical Green

At a Farmhouse East of Austin

We walked the fields that had been cleared
of cotton. Inside the weathered shed
I found a fist-sized snouted skull.

Back in the house, something other
than the heat is surely breathing.
Walls change their stains; the thin floor coughs.

I don't believe in ghosts. There's life
enough in what we live among
to keep our deepest doubts alive.

As night comes on, I lie awake
and wonder. Some seeds are cracking
open in the earth. The wind sings.

Tomorrow I'll return to what
I've made of city life. I'll bring
the skull and watch for its first bite.

Grackle, Like Steichen's Tree

Maybe when I get old
like Steichen you'll be

like his tree, there
beyond the window

in all kinds of
weather, your beak

like a dagger
looking for a heart,

your eye a piece
of frozen sun,

you or your stand-in
or his stand-in

clacking and whirring
and stalking a brown

companion, shoulder-
caped like some dracula,

indifferent to life
inside my room.

Buzzards

You'd think at fifty I might know
something about the way a car engine
works, or might want to know.
Gas and sparking, pistons, compression.
The guy thing, or Pirsig's balance
between cruising and carburation. I tried
to tune my Beetle years ago, pull at
the belts, follow electrical wires.
It didn't take. One of my college
students tells me he hates poems.
He can't make them make sense.
I tell him he'll have to read poems
to pass this course and get
a degree. Maybe he can learn
how to get behind the wheel,
start the poem up, and find
an image that can take him on
down the road, leaving the buzzards
to spiral along the refried roads,
waiting for heat strokes or road
kills, shimmering with symbolism.

Local Exotica

For an hour or two at dawn and dusk,
wild parrots wheel across our neighborhood,
ten or twelve strong, keen with squawking.

Like tropical green crosses with daggers
for tails, they settle into a halo of leaves,
bluster at grackles and doves, and scramble

back into the sky in ragged ranks, making
for a palm like the dead one at my house,
guarding nesting holes in pairs against woodpeckers.

Two blocks away at the zoo, people pay
good money to catch sight of scarlet macaws
and white cockatiels perched in the aviary.

The ones with the checklists, though, are out cruising
the *calles*, looking for a red or yellow headed
parrot, stalking our palms for a green parakeet,

kiskadee and green jay already spotted,
aplomado falcon and green kingfisher still at large,
life birds these birders hope to crow about.

One Evening Walking

One evening walking I saw something
in the street ahead, near the curb,
a dark shape like a glove, moving.
Or it seemed to be moving in the failing
light, move some and then stop,
as if on a string pulled bit
by bit by a little boy, the king
of the neighborhood. When I got
close I bent over to see better
and then stepped back, the hair
on my neck prickled by the hair
on the tarantula's black body,
the thought of that furry hand
springing up and seizing me
sending a shiver through both
arms and legs, no matter how much
I thought *harmless, harmless.*
I circled and went on, hoping
it wouldn't get flattened by a tire
but would find some damp spot
of dark as it moved from one dry
yard to another, a shadow of some
truth about houses and humans.

All the Young Swans

They tamped cotton
into bloody toeboxes

slathered antiperspirant
onto bare armpits

twisted hair into buns
behind feathered skullcaps

and floated to applause
across a lake of illusion.

Places of the Red Bike

Now that our son has found his pedals,
he is off to the places of the red bike.

Last spring I drove for days and days
deep into Mexico. Coastal roads were wretched,

riven by heavy rains. I saw some birds,
walked some ruins, lingered near Indians in Chiapas.

You are diving into childhood, where dreams
begin to take on form, take on a first

integument. Watch them as they shred
and flower, wheeling down each waning day.

South Texas Directive

This thirst at the throat
can't be slaked by the dust
and grit of the road
you've found yourself on.
Look where the birds go.
Then close your eyes and listen
to the scrub brush whisper,
whisper. Follow the aroma
of sound deeper than you'd
think you'd ever dare,
and there you may find
a pool to gargle in,
to go hip deep and sink
until you bubble like a fish,
a fat fish at rest at last,
eyes adjusting to each side
of the world, fins holding
everything equilibrious, gills
beginning to filter truth from fact.

Cicadas

Phil Spector's wall of sound sold lots of sixties' records,
but even Phil's no match for these cicadas,

their high-pitched drumming drone counterpointed
with strings of clicks, taking over the foreground

in early light, the air a swollen membrane rounder
than any rap song, an insect mantra growing

in the skull like a six-legged Buddha, sitting in his tree
with his 17-year smile and thousands of incarnations.

Elegy for Isaac Rosenberg, 1890-1918

It was the one we measure madness by,
the lines cutting across waves of farmland,
the bitter wires tearing out the tongues
of clerks and poets and neighborhood boys,
pungent gas no mustard plaster for the lungs:

where larks sang but no woman waited
for what the darkened night might bring,
where lice were all too intimate and shared
more than you could bear, the stretcher-bearer's
face flecked with a friend's wet brains:

it was no joke that first day of April,
just at dawn, struck down on night patrol,
an end to ruminations, verbal skirmishes,
eyes as cold as the sky, some German
boy wishing to be done soon too.

Birdwatching

From the window by his
desk, he watches birds.
His cat watches birds.

They have seen a brown
grackle sail onto the lawn.
She struts about, abugging.

Her perched mate staccatos
his clacks against the trees
and houses, man and cat.

The man wonders what meaning
the sounds make and where
the pair must roost at night.

The cat quickens, its hunting
rictus apulse, its eyes
full of feathers and flesh.

Startled by some sound or
movement, the brown grackle
disappears into a tree's crown.

The man looks at the cat.
The cat, relaxing, licks a paw.
Bird calls still puncture the air.

Tropical Green

This green goes deeper than the grin
on the face of the boy whose stare
his mother's voice soon calls home,
watching from the dark interior.

Deeper too than the tumble of words
in the market, where snatches of meaning
are lost in a cascade of syllables
that leave you wet but still thirsty.

So deep this green that it can choke
you in the night, its tendrils swelling
into ropes that wrap around your dreams
and take their breath away by light.

And still you stay a day longer, running
your hands along a pitted wall, drinking
the dark coffee in a thatched café, closing
your eyes to see a parrot's squawk more clearly.

From Flesh and Blood We Make Pie

He called it *quick* as it came on and clobbered
him, quicker than a gulf storm wave you turn

your back on for a breath that's gone in the tumble
of convulsive surf, the stagger back through

seaward suck fit tonic for abraded limbs, sweet
strawberries that sting of an old intimacy with air.

Too hard to tend a wound that's this deep and long
and sudden, the hot day cooling under the skin

like a pie congealing on the counter, food for ferocious
sacramental memories of what has come on a wave

of blood and gone on a wave of blood in what now
seems but a single slow-releasing gasp of time.

A Night in Guanajuato

remembering Wally Pierce

If we'd spent all our time gawking
at mummies, their leathery grins
hinting at some inside joke, and cruising
the shops for bargains, I'd have missed
what we found after the others gave out:

the inside of a bright cantina, the kind
with café doors and a urinal against
one wall, una cerveza y otra cerveza,
hoisting to the Irish on St. Paddy's,
the room thick with nighttime boister.

I sat con un amigo nuevo and stumbled
toward understanding, but when I turned
to the grumbling nearby, your face reddened
and ready for trouble, I knew the finger
poking your chest was untranslated provocation.

That we escaped with our tongues and our skin
was my stake in the skirmish, windsheeted
but not stupid, and arm in arm we returned
to our rooms, no better than the Irish,
no worse, destined to raise another day.

The News in Southern Colorado

Our jeep rocked up the private road,
kicking stones into the skinny creeks

we forded. When we got out, the hole
in the ragged rock wall nearby nearly winked.

Max steered us round his pristine stock pond,
gave out worms, gave out tips that settled

on the surface and then sank. We saw
the shapes, angled in that blue captivity,

we cast and let our bait sink till it
bobbered to a stop. "Don't pull it in,"

implored our guide, when, bored, we gave
our line a crank or two to tempt a trout,

German brown or rainbow. We hooked
our six apiece, as promised, and Dad

brought home the prize, five pounder
if an ounce – see him with Max,

two former newsmen, beaming
in the sunlight, the truth flashing

at the end of the line, easier
than it ought to be, really big news.

Mountains in June

At six this morning the mountains
above the western ridge have a noon
crispness, yet the others in the cabin
sleep on, carried by the river's
endless rush over rocks and logs
into the air's open stillness.

In a fir-and-pine, spruce-and-aspen
world, the news is nearly always
the same, but days of birds
and pine cones and wildflowers
can penetrate city folks' bones,
here where bears come at night
and leave word of their foraging
on pale tree bark, more electric
than any e-mail back home.

Fishing Morning

On fishing morning I rigged up my son's pole
and threaded a worm on, showed him
the eddy by the pipe that feeds the stream
under the road, and sat back and watched.

He snagged an overhanging tree, and then
caught brush at the eddy's edge.
His two cousins talked their way up and down
each bank, telling the trout their plans.

Well before lunch the boys were back inside
the cabin, taking turns with a battery-operated
fishing game, a stump of pole with a readout
and reel, hooking fish they'll never have to eat.

Communion

The snowmelt river below our cabin
a freeway of mountain memory,
its steady roar the sum of all
the sounds this forest has made.

Forty years ago we first visited
this valley, a Spanish spoon wedged
against mountains called Christ's blood,
the river its artery of salvation.

Now I'm older than my father then,
and he his mother, and my son
the I of the square Kodak photos
that still smell of Ponderosa pine.

We come back to break the body
and drink the blood of this earth,
to flex the family's muscle against
the trails into tomorrow's trees.

On a Hike along the Purgatoire River

We took the easy trail up the tumbling Purgatoire
toward Trinchera Peak, one eye peeled
for flowers, the other for signs of bear.

Red columbines, blue chiming bells. Bear scat
in a clearing by two tent-sized mounds of snow.
My son, stranger to such, leapt into a wet embrace.

Thirteen, still keen for our hugging, he lowers
his voice when his girlfriend phones. His upper lip
carries the shadow of his first mustache.

We share sandwiches and water on rocks
in the shade by the river. He leaves bread crusts
for the bears and strides off, radiant in his ignorance.

Words That Sound So Slow

The spokes off West Spanish Peak
speak volumes in volcanic undertone,
wheel of earthly fortune weathering
the spins of season, each spin
a needle of pine in this upstart
forest or flake of snow melting
into the infant roar of the river
that carved out the valley's tale,
retold by the choiring birds against
the sky, words that sound so slow
that I can only begin to imagine
what they must be meaning.

Laying Down Tracks

We crossed a boiling creek colder
than the snow it comes from,
our flatlander lungs pulling hard
for more ten-thousand-foot air,
and I sat outside the talk
and listened to the aspens
rustle aimlessly in the breeze,
the smaller trunks swaying as if
to the music of the mountain,
and with each breath the tang
of spring told the round of living,
the bittersweet taste in the teeth
defining all that we take in
as we lay down more tracks
for the wind and rain to scatter.

Where I've Come To

This is where I've come to,
this mountain pass, this marker,
this sky with rain clouds
building in the west,
the wind capable of cutting
the past into ribbons of regret,
the trees as thin and cold
as thoughts, the hawk along
the ridge focused on fur.
I stop and stake the tent,
swap boots for moccasins,
lie back against my pack,
and say the first words
of this day: *welcome home.*

When Gomez Paints

Clouds boil over. The sea boils up.
Best to fish then in the wind,

where light wiggles against the hook
of the mind, snags on jutting stumps

that might be the bones of the earth,
twisting around some fatal grip.

When it shatters, its flecks foam
into geometries of time, oranged

in the very green of blueness,
coating the world with silence.

Spring Again

Slow enough to find an old path
to a place that's been dry too long.

Time enough to wonder what the rain means,
slippery counterpoint to mockingbird talk.

Wet enough to wish new-planted roots
a way through mulched beds of clay.

Wait here for what you can't remember
yet: how the green leaves turn into birds.

Twenty Miles Inland

East wind brings fat fish on salted waves
that scour our houses, coat our private rooms.

Your walls full of flounder, fixed by gigs,
sidesaddle eyes aglow, spreading gossip about shrimp.

Here one swordfish, slick and fertile,
sawing through books for a spot on the shelf.

Come to my house, wear your muddy boots.
When our gills are red again we will slip

through the cracks of the floor and wiggle
our way eastward, finny for ice-cold anecdotes.

Living Salt Stew

Every day grows a little bit bigger
on the beach, the sky a fatter blue
and the gulls more nearly themselves.

I wake without words and heed the call,
ambling alongside diminishing spume,
listening for whatever I can take.

Ten stories up, and still the grinding sea
climbs through me as it rolls its tale inland,
a living salt stew that never stops for breath.

Forest of Air

Just try to rub the trees from your eyes,
this haze of particulate holding off the sun
and filling our lungs with leaf mold.

Slowly we are absorbed by this forest of air,
its silence buzzing with the final sounds of men
and animals a thousand miles south of here.

One day the wind will shift and the fires subside.
Only the dust will remember the Mayan dialect
and the long, resplendent feather of our shyest bird.

Going out to Come Back

Let light come early. What I've found
I cannot see to understand, cannot tell
by feeling where I've come to be.

You beside me – take my arm
and guide me to the door. No one else
will follow where I've got to go.

From tree to tree I hear the silence
of the dark, so long and loud it hurts the air
I'm breathing, gets inside my skin.

Is this the river? Once I learned
to walk and then to swim. If I can't touch
the bottom, can I find the top?

I can't remember when I started.
That's your voice I think I'm tasting –
last a little longer on my tongue.

Wait once more while I return.
Wet and foot sore, still I hope to hold
your eyes again until I sleep.

Another New Dance

Blood flakes, flutters off in a sudden gust.
Flesh lingers, then feeds the things that scrape
across the blackboards of our deepest fears.

The bones that are left are not the body.
With each star, each shift of sun to shade,
they dance lighter, and lighter, and lighter.

Where have they gone, those who have come
to a time of stillness, those who have found
that the world no longer awaits their whispers?

The air absorbs old smells, the earth the weight
of a foot, the wind the succession of words
that shape a single heart's long vibration.

Let the rains come and scrub the fingerprints
from the world's body, let it glisten with light,
let it rise and begin another new dance.

New Poems

Eye of the Beholder

They could be twins,
Semitic genes engineering
this moment of recognition
after centuries of separation,
their hearts taken whole
by prophetic visions turned
into cold convictions
playing out now as
bullets and bombs, and so
at this shopping mall
or crossroads checkpoint
they stare into each other's
eyes and find a reflection
of evil, their own shape
turned against themselves,
and beneath the horror
of explosion their blood
mingles as it seeps
into the dirt and asphalt
that give those left behind
the traction they think
they need to harden
resolve, reset the timer,
and run the tape again
and again and again.

Snapshot, 1969

I guess the fellow
in the photo
doesn't need to hear
where he's gone to,
what he's missed –

he's cold but satisfied,
arm in arm
with friends now dead
or disappeared,

the day's march
against the war
about to begin,

taking him
down a long trail
that's reached this house
and this image
in my hands.

Remembering Vietnam

Forty years ago I left good men
and a good ship and a bad war
in someone else's country, choosing

words over weapons, books over
battle stations. I still mourn
for the dead and the maimed,

and all those who live their losses
each time they reach to touch
a hand that is forever missing.

Drinking from the River

for Larry D. Thomas

Whether it's a torrent or a trickle
it's where you have to go

when you're thirsty and you
dip your cup and draw out

the clear tang and sip it first
and then take one long swallow.

An aftertaste of sky and stones
tree bark and feathered shadows

carves their names into logs
that you stack up one by one

against the failing light and let
the heat soak into your skin

and when you wake you can smell
the river beyond the scattered ashes.

Light of a Star

Today this poem means everything.
It is the bowl into which you place
a piece of star and the bark of an oak,
then grind them to a fine powder,
sweeten the mix with your blood,
and bake until brown and chewy.

Tomorrow this poem may mean nothing.
Who has time to stop and sort through
such images, the traffic already beginning
to clot, the radio news a mix of bloodshed
and political stagnation, someone honking
like a goose with its neck stuck in a noose.

So this poem reflects the light of a star
and fades, once again, as the sun rises.

One World

You said our Saskatoon friend and poet
wrote that a Native Indian's remains

are not those of some prehistoric hunter
of mastodons: "The frozen are our own."

That night you watched a string quartet
carve air into harmonic moments of joy,

the gritty words of outrage balanced
against the pure cries of the violin.

Back of the Envelope

You're the only one
who sends me
real letters these days

postage paid envelopes
turned inside out
cryptic notes enclosed

scribbled on today's back
your baseball epitaph
"Prince flops Jacoby soars."

The Exuberance of Snow

with a nod to Glen Sorestad

Flakes flutter around at first
and then the snow descends,
transforming bush and lawn
furniture, melting on the noses
of puzzled cats. By dark
when we exit a 3-D theatre
of jungle blue avatars our car
is blanketed and the windshield
iced over, first white Christmas
Eve in a century, here where
summers bake like unleavened bread.
We slush our slow way home
in a world lightened with false
promises that that night prove true.

In a Jar Suspended from a Branch

If you find this you will be close:
locate the tall pine by the boulder just ahead,
and go downhill until you reach a creek.
When you've crossed it, follow the marked trees
(I've chipped the bark at eye level)
up the rise, and when the ground flattens out
you'll see my cabin off to the left.
I say *my* cabin—whoever really owns it
stocked enough smoked meat and canned food
and coffee to last me long enough
for you to join me for a last meal here –
I hope. After we've eaten, I'll tell you
how I got separated from friends
on a hike last October and how I nearly
froze two nights before I crossed the creek
and found the cabin. Next day I fixed
coffee and stared out the front window,
and I could see two trails that took
different angles into the brush. But each
turned into tangles before I'd gone
a quarter mile or so, and all my yelling's
ever done is scatter birds and irritate
a napping bear or two. Once the snows
came, I've stuck close to home
and waited for someone to arrive.
Come soon, if you are coming, for
I'm running low on coffee, and when
it's gone I can only offer water
and my story, which gets colder
and colder as night comes on.

River Work

All night the narrow river outside this cabin
rumbles through my body, the cold current
penetrating the pores of mountain dreams
and scrubbing them against log and rock.

In the naked morning I wake to the possibilities
of light on the mountain, of air awash
with sound, of hunger in the belly,
of making the river's ripples out of words.

To Wildflower Season

One part could live in these mountains
from hibernation to wildflower season,

winding and unwinding like the roads
that bring supplies and tourists,

leathery skin craving the fat rains
of afternoon, first light of summer,

snow filling and unfilling the aspen gaps
all day, rustling the air with its secrets.

Colorado Hummers

Green wings awhir, female hummers zip
to and from the feeder, white tongues
draining the sugared water, slowly,
wary of the crimson-throated males
and their territorial zooms of jousting.

If these birds sipped snowflakes
instead and took on the nearby
mountain peaks, how long before
the high lakes would turn dry and
their rivers rage in rock and dust?

Mathematics of Meaning

He got so caught
in his tangle
of angles

that he couldn't
keep from growing
more obtuse

as he spoke
in circles
about triangles

and every hypotenuse
in the room
missed his point.

Spring Spawning on the Llano River

We pulled fish from the river
a hundred hours that day,
so many stringers of white bass
ogling the early evening sky,
outnumbering the stars
and their reflected winks,
their daily code of dying.

We pulled into a roadside store,
bought a box of 30-gallon bags,
iced down the vanload of fish,
then chewed through packets
of peanut butter crackers
and guzzled sodas on the way
back into the flickering city.

We pulled out thin knives
and carved flesh from bone
next morning, daylight thicker
in our burning eyes than even
the odor of gutted fish,
who will return in dreams,
wet, iridescent, uncatchable.

Shelf Life

It sits on a bookshelf
as if to swim across a sea
of words dammed up,
temporarily, inside their covers,
as if to offer its own story
of how liquid life infects
a Chinese carver and is
transformed by ancient stone
into a pop-eyed, pumpkin-
toned miniature that waits
with infinite patience
for the water to rise again.
On the other side of the shelf's
dividing wall, a glass cat
waits with infinite patience
for the first flicker of fin.

Whatever She Said

Whatever she said to him
must have been the wrong
thing, for him at least,
for though her cheeks were
streaked it was his heart
that took the verbal thrust,
each word twisting against
what he'd hoped for, and
then her sentences broke
off and he was left with
the hardest sounds buried
beneath the skin, bound
to work their way back
out, like shrapnel, over
the years to come, but until
then he'd feel their ache
whenever an inner wind
brought on cold weather.

Joker

The story was nearly familiar, the teller leaning back
in the booth and laughing hard enough to cause

those at nearby tables to turn our way, wondering
what sort of joke set off his outburst,

and we looked at him wonderingly too, his face
full of self-satisfaction, his loathing like a ghost

inside his language, a ghost of retribution
and self-loathing, the woman demonized and then

dismissed as if she could be gone so easily, as if
his clenching and unclenching hand told nothing more

than stiffness brought on by last night's cold front,
something an aspirin and hot shower could remedy.

Goldfish and Gravity

He said to her that the earth is as green
as a goldfish and as round as memory,

and she said to him that the heart is as stubborn
as a lie and as unforgiving as gravity.

His hope leaped anyway but fell as she began
to wiggle away, turning her round face once

and then disappearing from his green world
for good, leaving him only his rueful grin.

Letting the Animals Loose

Last night I let the animals loose,
domestic and wild, and while I slept
they wandered in and out of my dreams
and around the neighborhood, the smaller
ones keeping well wide of the bear,
the elephant wondering when the trick
would kick in. When the dark began
to dull toward day, each beast
had found its own place to be,
and in their dreams they waited
for a man to enter their territory
and make that one irreversible mistake.

Inland Sea

After words
disappear

gray salt soup
thickens

birds and fish
go too

rowing alone
in circles

at the edge
of sound.

Map Making

I've gone
from coffee

to moon
and back

enough times
to sketch

a map
of what

I've found
twinned in

the turn
from dark

to light
to dark

to light
to dark

to light.

Engine of Muscle

Serve off the sun
and come in,

geared for what
comes back quick,

the air all angles
and the heart

efficient as a
curt backhand

that clips the line
and ends game

and set and match,
such sweat so sweet.

American Pi

Take these ingredients –
pluck, idealism, savvy,
willfulness, hope, greed –

stir briskly and cover
with a latticed crust
of love crossing jealousy.

The distance from here
to there is fixed on maps
down to feet and inches,

but the arc of this life
defies a supercomputer's
digital reckoning.

No Hands

Short flight delay:
mechanical problem.

Then we board, taxi,
lift off, engines

rattling like baseball
cards against spokes,

bicycle pumping furiously
toward a cliff –

still our commuter jet
drones on and on,

shuddering its descent
into Little Rock,

and the boiling walk
to the gate ramp

is worth the damp
case of the wobblies.

The Way Home

From this height
quilted lily pads
stretch whitely

to the horizon
like ice floes
in the Arctic

and deeper down
shards of sea
wrinkle darkly

over land now
cotton bolls thin
as we bank

against the dusk
and glide into
our grounded selves.

In Flight

Inside this
sky-bound bullet
no one hears
the ticking down
of an unwound
heart, the cabin
light loosening
her thoughts and
streaming them
aft of the last
row of seats,
the air cold
as a dead
memory, while
far below the land
exhales slowly.

Approaching Shirazeh Houshiary's
Night of Ascension

At a distance you notice
a large frame squaring a small white disk
and its pale gray aura, tugging at your attention,
and as you come nearer a faint concentric web
emerges, drawing you further into the canvas,
pulling you toward its hole,
        and you think
momentarily of its counterweight out in space,
sucking everything in range into its infinite inkiness,
but here all is calm, off-white, the web a gentle swirl
of implication,
        and as a Westerner you begin
to wonder if, lurking just beyond one edge
of the canvas, a huge hairy-legged presence
hopes you will stay longer and become stuck
to the fine filigree that harbors the escape hatch,
just beyond your reach.

11:11

It has a balance I'd like
to achieve from day to day,
simple digits paired as morning
heads toward noon, doubly paired
and neatly colonized, as I aim
to follow routines, keep on track,
make marks on the face of time.
And later, well into the dark,
the doubled double digits light
the way to the end of the day,
tell me to sleep now, body
and mind yoked together, supine
as an old married couple,
arms relaxed along their sides,
snoring softly all the night long.

37

Better than pills or warm milk,
turn to a fine mid-range prime
number, strolling through your thoughts
in dark blue velvet, confident
in its drowsy articulations,
and as you follow its backward
breathing . . . thirty-six, thirty-five,
thirty-four . . . the night begins
to narrow into its tunnel . . .
thirty-two, thirty-one . . . taking
you deeper into a country
you've surveyed and populated,
and thirty thickly blurs into
twenty-nine, twenny-a, and
you're knee deep in a field
that climbs up and over hills
on the way to daybreak,
the place with its own time
and storehouse of colored shards
of memory, the strange zoo
of the possible and impossible,
and somehow the shoe you sailed
off in makes its return, full
of words and numbers you may
use once the sail is struck.

Invisible Arc

Poised at the edge like a diver
on the cliffs of Acapulco, the arc
of air almost visible, the sound
of waves against the rocks
as calming as his mom's humming,
he closes his eyes and bends
his muscular legs and stretches
wiry arms behind, ready to leap
from her eyes into what little
he knows of time's ice-blue depths
and the sinuous undertow of love,
pulling him out beyond the shore
where he will float with the rest
until at last he sinks from sight.

Onset

What fierce folds the heart's
accordion has:

a boy stretching
into his bearded being,

the playing field open
for unfolding dreams

that will dry like luck
next year or the next

while the road beyond
the field turns away

and disappears behind
the century's bend.

Fireflies in March

We watch
them wink

like stars
at sea

as we
blink back

to clay
midsummer ball

under lights,
Dad clapping

hope from
the dugout

while I
wait for

a pitch
to whack

through the
black hole

a firefly
leaves behind.

Yankee Bloodlines

The black-and-white photo frames
a ranch-style house and two boys
on the curb, with bat and glove
and ball caps on, pretending to be
waiting for The Mick to arrive
at his new Dallas home – that was
my brother and me, pulled from school
so the Times Herald photographer
could capture neighborhood spirit,
the shot picked up by papers
elsewhere in Texas and beyond.

I saw Mantle play once, at old
Yankee Stadium, early sixties:
he tripled into the monuments
in deep center, and I, just
recovering from an undetermined
childhood illness, not leukemia
as feared, gamely choking down
a mustard dog despite swollen
gums, filled in three corners
of the scorecard box. Then Howard
bounced to shortstop for out three.

Forty years later, my aunt buried
on a cold clear February day,
we gathered at her last stop,
assisted living New Canaan style,
for a final family commemoration.
A woman with a walker crossed
the room – Eddie Lopat's widow,

my cousin brightly noted, and
as we left she looked up and smiled,
a Yankee cap perched atop
white curls, jauntily incongruous.

Uncle Carroll Speaks

Uncle Carroll was born on July 13, 1919,
and died four months later, on November 15,
1919. His twin, Charles, died ninety-one
years later, on March 13, 2011.

On the Epidemic of 1918-1919

As we both got sicker that fall
Mother prayed and Dad swore
at the doctor, weary from sickbed
after sickbed and days of dying,
shaking his head slowly as if
the lamplight had brought on
a migraine, and later, as the flu
burned through the hollows
of my little body, the miracle they
hoped for quenched your thirst,
and I was left alone forever.
They say that when twins
in Africa become malnourished,
only one develops kwashiorkor,
listless and cantaloupe bellied,
like a green Pecos melon severed
from the vine, rotting in a field.
I'd like to give that child a bowl
of Mother's mashed pinto beans,
though they couldn't bring me back.

My Gifts

You could have been my mirror,
my right hand, my bunk bed
buddy. When the war came,
we could have both gone to sea,
two telepathic comm officers,
survivors. You would come back
to start a daily newsman's life,
while I could have written
the truth turned sideways, stories
of boys who scrabbled out of
West Texas and discovered
their authentic selves, or poems
of wonder, loss, love – poems
like this one, my precious brother,
poems I've never been able
to give you, gifts from a world
of could haves, might have beens.

Waiting for My Brother

You might think, all these years
gone, that my grudge against you
would have worn itself out,
victim of time's infinite erosions.
I know you were blameless,
barely surviving the viral assault
that seized that small frame house
by the throat and took just me
as its fatal prize. But you,
stubborn headed even then,
held on while I drifted, drowned.
Now, 91 years later, the days endless,
befogged, as you hold hands
with the woman who has shared
most of your life, I wait impatiently
for you to float into the ether
and, if I can find you, tell me
all that I missed, not being you.

Letter from the Void

None of you will ever know
which of us swam out first,
sputtering into the alien air,
giving up forever the gifts
of the womb for a tactile world
of uncertain hopes and certain death.
We were happiest floating
in our infinite universe,
neither hot nor cold, fingerlings
so fearless in our twinning.
You'd probably pick Charlie,
your father, Mr. Up at 5 A.M.,
Mr. Always Active and Organized,
as if he'd found his purpose
sooner than I had, as if he'd
pushed ahead to get the edge
on me, by those few minutes,
so when the flu finally found
our dusty Texas town that fall
he'd be the toughened one,
the favored one who stayed on,
the only son that would matter.
How do you know I wasn't first,
the more curious one, risking
all comfort to cry my shock
out loud, telling Charlie just what
lay ahead, and he, ever cautious,
had held back as long as he could,
letting me suffer in my scrawny
lonely nakedness until he had

to face his future too. But neither
of us can tell you now, and so,
if you should care, you'll have
to imagine which of us wanted
to be first, and why, and how
that's shaped what you've become.

My Regrets

I would have liked to marry a woman
like the one who picked you, brother, but mine
would have sung a sassy tune, a Texas
two step I could hum to from early coffee
to the last smooch at night, two kids, the whole
shebang. I think about what didn't happen
more than you ever thought about me,
I'm sure, the wind scouring your teen thirties,
then the long days of butchering cows and chickens,
then college, the good war, the quick marriage
that worked, three kids, the full career. And yet
I would give up my longest regrets
to sit beside you, shoulder to shoulder,
and say all those meaningless things that brothers
say when they mean everything to each other.

Constructing a Family

I wouldn't have needed so much –
a wife, for awhile at least,
a Texas gal I could stand
to share most days with,
at least until my headstrong son
and solipsistic daughter grew
out of adolescence and spoke
to me again. I'd have watched
you in my mind's eye, brother,
the way you kept an even keel,
and made sure that the cousins
made connections, links against
the steady corrosions of years,
though in the end it would be
up to them to say what love
held for those who shared
some of their same blood,
and I wish I could give you
photographs of those times
that I can only imagine,
faces and colors as fresh
as today's sunrise, but here
in the dark I now find
no images, no images at all,
only these memories, if what
these words make is of memory.

My Dream

These days I sometimes dream I've fathered
two sons, twins, who also bear our names,
and that they both have taken ill
when a sickness scoured our town,
and one lingers at the edge, then comes back,
and the other lingers for awhile
but slides away, like a fish back into water.
The one who lives is the one we named
Carroll, a thin baby, but tough
as barbed wire, and I tell my wife,
whose face I can't ever seem to form,
that our boy must be destined
to do something special, but the dream
ends then with the boy's smile
lighting his dark enigmatic eyes,
and there is no sequel.

At the River

When heat finally eased in September
we'd go down to Spring Creek
late in the afternoon, pecan trees
giving good shade, Mother holding
one of us and sister Babe the other,
and though we couldn't swim then,
bundled along the bank, we watched
the current ripple on toward the bridge,
free and easy like the lonesome crows
that crossed the yard all morning,
calling out to a big empty sky.
On toward dark they'd take us home,
a spare frame house letting hot air
leak out of wide-open windows,
and we'd commence to crying then,
our bellies empty and sorrowful,
begging Mother for early dinner,
our steady sucking turning time
into its own glowing fullness,
and then Babe would slowly rock us
in Dad's homemade double cradle
until the lamplight flickered
and failed and we drifted
like leaves into the undulating
waves of the night, a short dying
before the long and final one.

The Thunderstorm

My dreaming ended with a sharp
crack and an even louder *boom*,
and when something began to hammer
the whole house faster and harder,
my brother and I both started
wailing, and Mother got up out of
the dark and pulled us right
into her warm smell as she made
her way into the front room,
found the chair, and rocked
us back and forth while Dad
lit the lamp and set a bucket
near the stove to catch the rain
that was dripping from the ceiling,
and when I got used to the heavy
drumming I closed my mouth,
and my brother did too, and after
a long time the windows took on
light and the racket began to ease,
and as Dad worried about the sheep
Mother said they had more sense
than most people did and then laid us
into the double cradle, thanked
the Lord for the rain, and started
cooking breakfast, and the smell
of the rain filled our house all day,
and when it finally evaporated,
it was gone from me forever.

Speaking of Language

I first came to learn language
as I floated with my brother
for month after month, Mother's
words vibrating into our hearts,
inside her warm, infinite womb,
and after we were expelled
from paradise and forced to face
the pitiless daylight and all
its petty cacophonous boasting,
I listened to other nearby voices,
Dad's and my sister's, absorbing
their intonations, their inflections,
and started to shape my gurgles
into approximated syllables,
feeling my way through the air.
Now all I have are words, words
for blood and bone and touch,
words for laughter and sorrow,
words for the love I once felt
and still listen for, as the wind
brings only the faintest sounds
of the disembodied world beyond.

Night Talk

I heard them talking on into the dark
about the sun burning through the day,
and what they needed to do to pay for
eggs and meat to make the beans stretch,
three mouths to feed and two more
still nursing like hungry calves,
farming cotton and tending to the sheep,
young and strong and stuck in love,
hoping that their luck would click
into gear and grind them onward,
hour after hour, day after day,
our empty wails the spurs to all
their finest hopes and simplest
beliefs, that with the light of dawn
they would rise from bed and begin
again, and somehow they'd provide
what we needed, blind to what
would strike like a snake and take
me away, lost forever as when night
swallows day's final breath of light.

At the Sherwood Cemetery

So you've come to this graveyard
to find a headstone with my name
chiseled out. Listen to the windmill
inside the entrance, creaking
and groaning all day and night,
and you'll likely learn as much
as you will by walking up
and down these rows, though
there are other Damerons about
and even a section of Millses,
my mother's people. I should
have been buried here back then,
chilly day in November, small
cheap casket, some flowers, a couple
of dozen relatives, but where
exactly is anybody's guess.
See those flat chipped stones
with rocks a body's length
away, or a long arm's?
Lots of these dead are lost
to language, now, the wind
their only inscription. Maybe
you can hear my name
if you listen closely, but
you'll never ever know where
my small bones lie, forever apart
from my twin brother, buried
ninety years later with a fine
bronze marker in Big D.,
so people won't forget him
like they have me.

Remembering Their Departure

The wind whistled through this graveyard
like a distant train back then, just
as it does now. After I was buried,
Mother came by pretty regularly,
sat on the dry grass, talked about
things that'd happened day to day.
My sister Babe watched my twin at home.
One day Mother said they were heading west
for Texon and the Big Lake oil field,
my five-year-old twin happy to bounce
toward prosperity in their 1913 Tin Lizzie.
I kept waiting for their return.
Two years later they went on to McCamey,
further west, feeding oilfield workers
(and gamblers, bootleggers, and prostitutes)
at their café, then lodging them
at Dad's self-built rooming house.
And so the wind whispered the years
away, decade by decade, and every one
of them is gone, but I'm still here,
waiting for one of them to come back
and tell me what life is all about.

Acknowledgments

Grateful acknowledgment goes to the following publications where various of these poems appeared, in some cases in slightly different forms:

Abbey, Aethlon, Bird Watcher's Digest, Borderlands, Borders Review, Boundless, Cedar Rock, The Chronicle of Higher Education, Concho River Review, Confluencia/Convergence, Creeping Bent, Culebra, Descant, El Rocinante, The Formalist, Gryphon, Hayden's Ferry Review, Higginson Journal, Innisfree, International Poetry Review, Iron Horse Literary Review, Lucille, Mesquite Review, Midland Review, Mississippi Review, The Modern Rhapsode, New Century North American Poets, New Poetry Appreciation, New Texas, Okike, The Old Red Kimono, Parnassas Literary Review, Pax: A Journal for Peace through Culture, Poetic Space, Puerto del Sol, Pushing the Envelope: Epistolary Poems, RE:AL, The Redneck Review of Literature, Red River Review, Roanoke Review, Salome, Southern Ocean Review, Southwestern American Literature, Stardancer, Sulphur River Review, Tar River Poetry, Taos Review, Terrapin, Texas College English, Texas in Poetry: A 150-Year Anthology, Texas Quarterly, Thicket, Writer's Bloc, 90 Poets of the Nineties: An Anthology of American and Canadian Poetry.

About the Author

Chip Dameron is the author of seven collections of poetry and a travel book. His poems and essays on contemporary writers have appeared in such periodicals as *Mississippi Review, Southwestern American Literature, San Pedro River Review, Puerto del Sol, Hayden's Ferry Review, New Orleans Review, Texas Quarterly*, and many other journals and anthologies, as well as publications in Canada, Ireland, Nigeria, India, China, Thailand, and New Zealand.

Dameron has co-edited two literary magazines, *Thicket* and *Chachalaca Poetry Review*, and served on the editorial board of four others. A two-time nominee for the Pushcart Prize in poetry and a member of the Texas Institute of Letters, he lives and writes in Brownsville, Texas.

Wings Press was founded in 1975 by Joanie Whitebird and Joseph F. Lomax, both deceased, as "an informal association of artists and cultural mythologists dedicated to the preservation of the literature of the nation of Texas." Publisher, editor and designer since 1995, Bryce Milligan is honored to carry on and expand that mission to include the finest in American writing—meaning all of the Americas, without commercial considerations clouding the decision to publish or not to publish.

Wings Press intends to produce multi-cultural books, chapbooks, ebooks, recordings and broadsides that enlighten the human spirit and enliven the mind. Everyone ever associated with Wings has been or is a writer, and we know well that writing is a transformational art form capable of changing the world, primarily by allowing us to glimpse something of each other's souls. We believe that good writing is innovative, insightful, and interesting. But most of all it is honest.

Likewise, Wings Press is committed to treating the planet itself as a partner. Thus the press uses as much recycled material as possible, from the paper on which the books are printed to the boxes in which they are shipped.

As Robert Dana wrote in *Against the Grain*, "Small press publishing is personal publishing. In essence, it's a matter of personal vision, personal taste and courage, and personal friendships." Welcome to our world.

Colophon

This first edition of *Drinking from the River*, by
Chip Dameron, has been printed on 55 pound
Edwards Brothers Natural Paper containing a
percentage of recycled fiber. Titles have been
set in Cochin type, the text in Adobe Caslon
type. All Wings Press books are designed and
produced by Bryce Milligan.

On-line catalogue and ordering:
www.wingspress.com

Wings Press titles are distributed
to the trade by the
Independent Publishers Group
www.ipgbook.com
and in Europe by
www.gazellebookservices.co.uk

Also available as an ebook.